TO GOD

BE THE

GLORY

TODAY'S
ISSUES

TO GOD

BE THE

GLORY

JOHN D.
HANNAH

CROSSWAY BOOKS • WHEATON, ILLINOIS
A DIVISION OF GOOD NEWS PUBLISHERS

Published by Crossway Books
 a division of Good News Publishers
 1300 Crescent Street
 Wheaton, Illinois 60187

First printing, 2000

Printed in the United States of America

ISBN 1-58134-171-7

The Alliance of Confessing Evangelicals exists to call the church, amidst our dying culture, to repent of its worldliness, to recover and confess the truth of God's Word as did the Reformers, and to see that truth embodied in doctrine, worship, and life.

Library of Congress Cataloging-in-Publication Data
Hannah, John D.
  To God be the glory / John Hannah.
    p.   cm. — (Today's issues)
  Includes bibliographical references.
  ISBN 1-58134-171-7 (trade pbk. : alk. paper)
    1. Glory of God. 2. God—Worship and love. I. Title. II. Today's issues (Wheaton, Ill.)
BT180.G6 H36 2000
248.3—dc21   99-045158
                                                                    CIP

| 15 | 14 | 13 | 12 | 11 | 10 | 09 | 08 | 07 | 06 | 05 | 04 | 03 | 02 | 01 | 00 |
| 15 | 14 | 13 | 12 | 11 | 10 | 9 | 8 | 7 | 6 | 5 | 4 | 3 | 2 | 1 | |

CONTENTS

PREFACE

These are not good days for the evangelical church, and anyone who steps back from what is going on for a moment to try to evaluate our life and times will understand that.

In the last few years a number of important books have been published all trying to understand what is happening, and they are saying much the same thing even though the authors come from fairly different backgrounds and are doing different work. One is by David F. Wells, a theology professor at Gordon-Conwell Theological Seminary in Massachusetts. It is called *No Place for Truth*. A second is by Michael Scott Horton, vice president of the Alliance of Confessing Evangelicals. His book is called *Power Religion*. The third is by the well-known pastor of Grace Community Church in California, John F. MacArthur. It is called *Ashamed of the Gospel*. Each of these authors is writing about the evangelical church, not the liberal church, and a person can get an idea of what each is saying from the titles alone.

Yet the subtitles are even more revealing. The subtitle of Wells's book reads *Or Whatever Happened to Evangelical Theology?* The subtitle of Horton's book is *The Selling Out of the Evangelical Church*. The subtitle of John MacArthur's work proclaims, *When the Church Becomes Like the World*.

When you put these together, you realize that these careful observers of the current church scene perceive that today evangelicalism is seriously off base because it has abandoned its evangelical truth-heritage. The thesis of David Wells's book is that the evangelical church is either dead or dying as a significant religious force because it has forgotten what it stands for. Instead of trying to do God's work in God's way, it is trying to build a prosperous earthly kingdom with secular tools. Thus, in spite of our apparent success we have been "living in a fool's paradise," Wells declared in an address to the National Association of Evangelicals in 1995.

John H. Armstrong, a founding member of the Alliance of Confessing Evangelicals, has edited a volume titled *The Coming Evangelical Crisis*. When he was asked not long afterwards whether he thought the crisis was still coming or is actually here, he admitted that in his judgment the crisis is already upon us.

The Alliance of Confessing Evangelicals is addressing this problem through seminars and conferences, radio programs, *modern* REFORMATION magazine, Reformation Societies, and scholarly writings. The series of booklets on today's issues is a further effort along these same lines. If you are troubled by the state of today's church and are helped by these booklets, we invite you to contact the Alliance at 1716 Spruce Street, Philadelphia, PA 19103. You can also phone us at 215-546-3696 or visit the Alliance at our website: www.AllianceNet. org. We would like to work with you under God "for a modern Reformation."

James Montgomery Boice
President, Alliance of Confessing Evangelicals
Series Editor, Today's Issues

ONE

A Radical Perspective

Not long ago I was in a certain church for the beginning of a worship service. With exuberance and uplifted hands, the choir called us to "celebrative" worship by singing, "I feel good." I was profoundly disturbed because it seemed to me that such a call to worship is saying that we do not really need to come to God and that he should appreciate it when we take time from our busy schedules to recognize his existence. By contrast, the validity of true religious faith and the reason for gathering corporately is to celebrate the glories of God while confessing his grace toward us in the adoration of his person.

Many churches have fallen prey to cultural assimilation. They have degenerated into self-serving enterprises whose primary celebration is to exalt God as giver and the validation of a message of cultural narcissism and personal advantages. Such churches have accommodated themselves to things that are not eternal. Genuine worship is not like that. It realizes the worth of God and our dependence on him. It is not a celebration of a favored socioeconomic status within a decadent capitalistic state.

Any sane person might tip his allegorical hat to a God who is merely a cosmic provider, but Christian communities do not exist to wonder at their physical abundance. They exist to adore the God who is abundant in mercy and forgiveness.

The Erosion of God-Centeredness

Forces set in place since the seventeenth century have created a downward spiral of life and values in western culture. A focus on God and his Word has a liberating effect on people, but a departure from the Word with an emphasis on self leads to bondage. With roots in the Enlightenment, which emphasized the supremacy of reason or natural revelation, the Modern Age (1750-1900) stressed human perfectibility through education and advances in science while denying the biblical doctrine of human insufficiency. The rationality of mankind became the hope of what was thought to be an ever-improving, increasingly benevolent world. This view of the world and life collapsed under the weight of contrary evidence. Several world wars and mass genocides have told us that while advances in science can improve life in many wonderful ways, secular education cannot and does not improve the dark side of the human species. In fact, increasing knowledge can make it even darker and more dangerous.

The Modern Age has ended. However, what replaced it was not a return to the biblical world of the first century or the Reformation of the sixteenth century but human despair. The Modern Age embraced the possibility of corporate cohesiveness through a common moral perspective, but that proved to be a myth, and what replaced it was an emphasis on the self, personal rights, and private morals. Thus was born the Postmodern Age with its call to radical self-centeredness.

The fruit of postmodernity has been a re-visioning of society. Social commentators have warned of this, from the secularist Christopher Lasch (*The Culture of Narcissism*, 1969) and the

Christian apologist Francis Schaeffer to a litany of recent writers such as George Barna, Michael Horton, and David Wells. Among its many manifestations are these:

1. *A trivialization of values.* This flows from our consumerism, the gathering of wealth, and a preoccupation with sports and leisure. Americans live for the passing tantalization of mere pleasures, while public virtues crumble into the abyss of private, individual values.

2. *Self-absorption and self-centered living.* As monitored by our social conversations, we seem to value athleticism (the virtue of strength), physical beauty (the art of temporal attractiveness), and money (portfolios and retirement packages) above everything, not concern or sacrifice for others.

3. *A loss of thankfulness.* Preoccupied with ourselves, we have lost the grace of being thankful. It is sad to live in a world where there is no one to thank because we have ourselves become the cause and source of all good things.

In light of these trends, it is little wonder that many of our churches lack a serious call to the worship of God. What is lacking is not structure in worship. All churches have that. Rather, it is heartfelt contriteness and humility in worship. God's perspective on worship has been left out, and that cannot be restored without renewing our focus on God.

The Reformation Model

There is no better model for the church today than that based on the biblical principles seen in the sixteenth-century Protestant Reformation. Martin Luther, John Calvin, and a host of other Reformers called for radical God-centeredness as the essence of genuine Christian profession and life. Their view of the faith was so radically different from that of much contemporary Christendom, and so thoroughly biblical, that a return from the emptiness of a Christianity shaped by postmodern values to a Reformation faith based on the Scriptures would go a long way toward the renewal of our churches today.

The Reformation was a call for authentic Christianity, an attempt to escape the medieval corruption of the faith through renewal and reform. Its teaching, which swirled around a fivefold repetition of the word *sola* ("alone"), was a radical message for that day (and should be for ours) because it called for a commitment to an entirely God-centered view of faith and life.

1. *Scripture alone.* The Reformers insisted, as the foundation of everything else, that the Scriptures alone are 1) the authority in all matters of faith and practice, 2) the content of God's revelation to mankind, and 3) from the One who is incapable of deception or being deceived. God alone is true, and his Word is a product of the perfections of his character. Therefore, it alone is entirely true and trustworthy.

2. *Christ alone.* The Reformers insisted that Christ alone is the Redeemer. They understood by this that: 1) Christ alone is the means of salvation; 2) the ground of redemption is nothing other than the work of Christ at Calvary, making a penal satisfaction by offering himself to God for sinners; and 3) to do this he must be God's unique Son or equal, since God's character demands a payment that meets the demands of his own being, and no mere creature could ever supply that.

3. *Grace alone.* The Reformers insisted that the inability of the creature to cause God to reveal himself in anything but just wrath meant that salvation must be by grace alone, without any human merit to effect it. Such a radical, though quite biblical, understanding of the Bible meant that God alone provides salvation. It cannot be won by human merit.

4. *Faith alone.* The Reformers insisted that sal-

vation was through faith alone. Faith is not the cause of God's grace. It is our response to the revelation of God's grace to the soul. This means: 1) Faith is not meritorious, being only the means of appropriating God's provision of mercy in Christ; 2) faith is our embracing of what Christ has already done for us, not the cause of it; and 3) faith is itself a gift from God.

5. *Glory to God alone.* The fifth point is the focus of this booklet—the glory of God alone. It is the logical implication of the other four points, a call to a radical vision of God-centered living in all of life's many facets. The glory of God alone implies the right purpose for all of life—a God-centered purpose. All who share this radical view of Christianity make God's glory the ultimate purpose of life, not their own self-fulfillment or self-realization.

To Be God-Centered

There is no better summary of "the glory of God alone" than Paul's statement in Romans 11:36: "For from him and through him and to him are all things. To him be the glory forever! Amen." This is Paul's justification for a profoundly God-centered approach to life. The fourfold repetition of "him" within the compass of these few words illumines the central and exclusive focus for the Christian— God and his glory. Furthermore, the reason for this radical vision of life is expressed in three prepositions—"from," "through," and "to."

The first of these words, "from," indicates that God is the *source* of all things. All things have their origin or cause in God. This is in harmony with the statement of John the evangelist: "Through him all things were made; without him nothing was made that has been made" (John 1:3). All things come from God. The uncreated made everything created.

The second of these words, "through" (or

"by"), indicates that God is the *sustainer* of all he created. That is, the existence of creation depends upon the every-moment benevolence of God. Paul wrote of Jesus, "He is before all things, and in him all things hold together" (Col. 1:17). The uncreated not only made all things. He sustains them even now by the word of his power.

The third of these words, "to" (or "for"), indicates the *goal* of all that God created. All things were made by God, and all things exist for him. He who created all things is the end for which all things were made. In these expressions Romans 11:36 presents an orientation to life that is radically opposed to the values and pleas of modern culture. It is this God-centered view of life that I want to define and explain in this booklet.

TWO

The Glory of God:
Its Meaning

The chief Old Testament word for glory is *kavod,* and the main New Testament word is *doxa.* There are several significant nuances as these words are applied to God in the Bible. For example, glory is used to express God's internal qualities or attributes. It refers to such *essential aspects of his being* as excellency, dignity, worthiness, greatness, or beauty. In this sense the term implies being weighty (a literal meaning of *kavod*), much like some people today speak of something that is important to them as being "heavy."

Another important use of the term is *the display or shining out of God's internal qualities.* Used this way, "glory of God" can imply a visible exhibition, an effulgent brightness, or a display of his excellencies. Ezekiel was using the word this way when he wrote, "I saw the glory of the God of Israel coming from the east. His voice was like the roar of rushing waters, and the land was radiant with his glory" (Ezek. 43:2).

In the Scriptures, the phrases "name of God" and "glory of God" are often used synonymously. In Psalm 8:1 David wrote, "O Lord, our Lord, how majestic is your name in all the earth! You have set your glory above the heavens." Used this way, God's name can refer both to his internal qualities and to the revelation or exhibition of them. In Exodus

33:19 God told Moses, "I will cause all my goodness to pass in front of you, and I will proclaim my
name, the LORD, in your presence."

God's Glory, God's Ultimate End

For many of us who have been influenced by the
Westminster Shorter Catechism, the first question,
"What is the chief end of man?" has had a life-shap-
ing effect on how we have come to view God and
our world. I would propose a similar question
here—namely, "What is the chief end or purpose of
God?" Why did God create the world and
mankind? I answer: God's chief end is to be known
in all his glory.

The words "chief end" (or "ultimate end")
suggest a purpose in light of which there are no
other purposes—that is, the final and conclusive
end of all things. God's chief end in the creation
could not have been the creation itself, because the
world would then have to have been eternal and
equal with God. Since the world is not eternal but
an effect caused by the power of God, it could not
be the ultimate end of itself. This would lift an
effect into the realm of pure cause, a cause that we
know is God alone. It would be making a sec-
ondary cause into a final cause. Jonathan Edwards,
the eighteenth-century Puritan thinker, saw this
and argued rightly:

> That perfection of God which we call faith-
> fulness, or his inclination to fulfill his
> promises to his creatures, could not prop-
> erly be what moved him to create the
> world, nor could such a fulfillment of his
> promises to his creatures be his last end in
> giving the creatures being. ("The End for
> Which God Created the World, in *The
> Works of Jonathan Edwards* [Yale edition],
> 8:412; for a reprint of this great work by

Edwards and insightful commentary on it, see John Piper's *God's Passion for His Glory: Living the Vision of Jonathan Edwards* [Wheaton, Ill.: Crossway Books, 1998])

How are we to discover the final end for which God created all that has been created? Natural knowledge and human faculties cannot solve such a question because, assuming that the answer lies in God himself, God is beyond the grasp of natural knowledge. The only way we can know the end for which God created all things is to depend on the revelation of God in the Bible, the only infallible source of all true wisdom.

Why then did God create the world? And why did he create mankind to inhabit it? It is illogical to think that an all-sufficient God created the world because of some personal need or internal inadequacy. There is no inadequacy in God. God is perfect in all his being and in all his ways. He is infinitely glorious and unchangeably happy. He has no need of improvement. God could not better his own perfection or see a need to. It would mean that God was not perfect before he did so.

Because creation could not have been required by any cause outside of God, God being uncaused and unmovable, the cause must lie within the being of God himself. The very nature of God's being, that is, he alone, is the cause of his creative activities. It might be explained this way. God values himself above all else, and because he does, he is himself the end of creation. When the world is consumed in the final judgment and time will no longer exist, the ultimate end of God's handiwork will be known. It will be evident then that God is the final end of all his activities.

In God's being rightly consumed by his own glorious perfections and by delighting in himself, we have the answer to the question, What moved

God to create things when there was no external need for him to do so? In God, being is doing. Thus, being perfect is to will perfection. No external power could have caused God to act. Rather, his own overflowing nature and his delight in the revelation of his nature caused it. Because of who God is, God could not simply *be* powerful, holy, faithful, and true. He needed to exude these qualities. Thus the ultimate end of creation lies not in creation but in the Creator himself.

Edwards stated the point succinctly: "If the world had not been created, these attributes [justice, power, goodness, and wisdom] never would have any exercise" ("The End for Which God Created the World," p. 429).

God's love for himself is the clue to creation's true purpose. In other words, God created the world to reveal himself. There is, then, a property in God's being that not only delights in himself but longs to show himself. We might say that there is a divine self-love in God. But unlike the display of narcissism in God's creatures, this self-love is not sinful, for God's delight in himself is not a vain misconception. It is just and right. Said Edwards, "If it is fit that God's power and wisdom . . . should be exercised and expressed in some effects, and not lie eternally dormant, then it seems proper that these exercises should appear, and not be totally hidden and unknown" ("The End for Which God Created the World," p. 431).

God created in order "to show his supreme respect for himself," not for the creation in a final sense. Simply put, what God most values he has a right to reveal, and what he most values is himself. Against the shallow, self-centered culture in which we live, this radically biblical view offers hope by saying that there is something infinitely better than a preoccupation with our own personal gain and happiness. Finite visions of the purposes of God are all ultimately unsatisfying.

Stephen Charnock, the great Puritan divine, summarized the point of this section when he wrote:

> The reason that induced [God] to create must be of as great an eminency as himself: the motive could not be taken without him, because there is nothing but himself in being. . . . Again, the end of every agent is that which he esteems good, and the best good for that kind of action. Since nothing is to be esteemed good but God, nothing can be the ultimate of God but God himself and his own goodness. . . . God cannot will anything as his end of acting, but himself, without undeifying himself. (*The Existence and Attributes of God,* [Carlisle, Pa.: Banner of Truth Trust], pp. 228-229)

Objections Answered

There is a section in "The End for Which God Created the World" in which Edwards suggests possible objections to this radical theistic approach to the meaning of creation. His answers elucidate the point that God himself is the center and goal of all his works, not the creature.

Here are the objections Edwards addresses:

1. *If God is above all need of being added to or advanced in any way, if God is made not better or happier by anything, why would he will to create in the first place?*

Edwards answers that although God is not profited by creation, he does admire his own reflection in creation. God's pleasure is in seeing not his creation in itself but rather himself in his creation. Edwards wrote, "This is the necessary consequence of his delighting in the glory of his own nature, that he delights in the emanation and effulgence of it" ("The End for Which God Created the World," p. 447). If God is completely satisfied in himself, why should he desire something more? Edwards replies that although God needs no greater pleasure than he already has in himself, the pleasure of beholding his perfect wisdom and manifesting his power necessitates creation. God does not gain from beholding himself in any material or spiritual sense. He merely likes to view the perfection that is himself alone.

2. *If God receives praise from his creatures when they reflect God's nature back upon himself, is this not the vanity of seeking popular applause?*

Edwards's reply is that the desire of praise is not itself evil. It is sin only when the desire for praise is rooted in unworthiness. This is not the case with God since praise accorded to him is entirely just and right. Edwards writes, "A being that loves himself, necessarily loves love to himself. If holiness in God consists chiefly in love to himself, holiness in the creature must chiefly consist in love to him. And if God loves holiness in himself, he must love it in the creature" ("The End for Which God Created the World," p. 456).

3. *Because this understanding of God's purpose in creating the world flows from his very nature, doesn't it take away God's freedom to act without necessity?*

Edwards discusses this issue extensively in other places, but the essence of his reply is to define freedom as the ability of anyone to choose willingly or act voluntarily. Freedom is not the ability to choose contrary to what one desires but to choose in accordance with it. Since God delights in beholding his own glories and freely desires to do so, God is without necessity or external force in doing so. He acts with full freedom when he delights in himself. In fact, since freedom is the ability to act in conformity to one's nature, God is actually the most free of all beings since he alone is utterly powerful and altogether perfect.

This understanding of God and of the meaning and worth of life is radical in our postmodern, self-oriented society. It is a relentless God-centered outlook on the whole of life. Why are we here? What are we to do in these passing days? The Bible gives an answer to these and many similar questions that is distinctly different from what our secular contemporaries are saying. The Bible teaches that self is not the center. Life is not about a lakefront home, extensive vacations, or an early retirement. It is about who God is, what his interests and desires are, and how we can bring our lives into conformity to him. We are happiest when we live in conformity to God's desires for us.

John Piper calls this outlook the "continental divide" in theology. "If you really believe this," he says, "all the rivers of your thinking run toward God. If you do not, all the rivers run toward man. . . . Settling this issue is worth many nights of prayer and months of study" (*God's Passion for His Glory*, p. 141, note 21).

THREE

The Glory of God:
The Purpose of Creation

According to the secular viewpoint, the world was made by a series of natural causes, and our purpose in life is to maximize our enjoyment while minimizing discomfort. The only option in this meaningless world is to exploit things and people because self is the center of life. This approach is captured pathetically in such popular commercial catchphrases as "You deserve a break today," "You only go around once," and "I'm worth it." This calculated abandonment to naturalism has fractured our cultural morals and now threatens to bring chaos into our families, schools, communities, and government. Its fruit is not freedom but the unforgiving and unrelenting chains of violence and bondage that we see all around us. Without law, which presupposes a lawgiver, there can be no true freedom.

Our only hope is to return to the God of the Scriptures and the truth that the center of all meaning in life is not ourselves but God. God is the center of the universe and the essence of all wisdom and all truth. The purpose of life derives from God's desire to see his own glory and behold his own beauty. Thus it is time for Christians to be called back to the truth that the meaning of life is to be found in "the glory of God alone."

God's Glory and the Physical World

The psalmist proclaimed, "The earth is the LORD's, and everything in it, the world, and all who live in it" (Ps. 24:1). It is a fundamental truth of the Scriptures that God made the world. That is, it emerged by the actions of a creative mind and not as a product of the unexplainable concurrence of any number of natural events over an extended period of time. Psalm 33:6 sets forth the magnificent and effortless actions of God in speaking forth the creation: "By the word of the LORD were the heavens made, their starry host by the breath of his mouth."

Why did God create our world? For what purpose did the Lord speak physical complexity into existence? We discussed this in the previous chapter, but because of its enormous importance we will now consider the topic further.

1. *The world was made to teach those who live in it that there is a Creator.* It is a "book" that instructs those who "read" it that there is a God who fashioned it out of nothing. Calvin spoke of creation as a "school room" where we are taught (*Institutes of the Christian Religion* [Philadelphia: Westminster, 1960], 1, 4, 6). Edwards called creation "the voice of God" that instructs us in heavenly truths ("Images of Divine Things," *Works*, 11:74).

2. *God created the world to reveal aspects of his character.* Though "now we see through a glass, darkly," the world about us nevertheless reveals the ways and being of God. The creation is a wordless book that offers us images of profoundly wonderful truths revealed in the Bible. Edwards wrote much about the corollaries between the natural world and divine revelation. For example, "As all the world is enlightened and brought out of darkness by the rising of the sun, so by Christ's rising we are begotten again to a living hope" ("Images of Divine Things," *Works*, 11:66). Simply stated,

"Natural things were ordered for types of spiritual things" ("Images," 11:62).

3. *God created the world to display his excellencies.* This was not merely for the creatures to behold but for himself to see. God made the world for himself supremely, though, as in all his works, there are profound and wonderful benefits for the creation. The beauty and perfections of the physical world were intended to mirror the beauty and perfections of God. So in the beholding of himself God is glorified. Using a text such as Revelation 1:8 ("I am the Alpha and the Omega"), Edwards argued that since Christ is the beginning and end of all things, the end is therefore the same as the beginning with God. Since we know that when the end of creation comes all will give themselves to the praise and adoration of God, it must be for the praise of God that the world was created.

God's Glory and the Creation of Mankind

If the supreme divine purpose of creation was for it to be a mirror reflecting the perfections of its Creator, the ultimate purpose of God's highest form of creative activity—making mankind—must be the same. God did not make men and women so they could spend their time and creative energies on themselves. They were made to reflect in their characters and activities the very character and activities of God. By manifesting the purpose of our creation, we honor our Creator. We have been made to mirror God's holiness and righteousness back to God, not so *we* may benefit (though there are immeasurable benefits to personal godliness), but so God will be glorified in beholding himself in his creatures.

The Scriptures abound with statements about God's glory being the ultimate reason for the creation of mankind. Through Isaiah, God spoke of "everyone who is called by my name, whom I created for my glory, whom I formed and made" (Isa. 43:7). Speaking of the final restoration of mankind later in the same book, God says that he will do it "for the display of his splendor" (Isa. 61:3). Similarly, God indicates that he is jealous of his glory: "For my own sake, for my own sake, I do this. How can I let myself be defamed? I will not yield my glory to another" (Isa. 48:11).

Thus, God created us so he could see himself in us. In seeing himself in mankind, he is pleased. His pleasure is not in the creature per se, but in his own character revealed through the character of the creature. This is a radical, God-centered view of our purpose, not a self-oriented perspective on it. Edwards said it well: "In the creature's knowing, esteeming, loving, rejoicing in and praising God, the glory of God is both exhibited and acknowledged; his fullness is received and returned" ("The End for Which God Created the World," p. 531).

Speaking of Edwards's view of mankind relative to God's supreme purpose in creation, John E. Smith has written:

> God wants out of the depths of his love to have in creation a being capable of appreciating the beauty . . . and splendor of the divine *gloria* as it appears in creation. It is in this sense that Edwards understood God's end in creation as the full manifestation of his own glorious nature; what better way to achieve this end than through the person of true virtue whose life, imbued with grace and the divine Spirit, shines forth with the fullness of holy love and practice. (*Jonathan Edwards* [South Bend, Ind.: Notre Dame Press, 1992], p. 107)

David wrote, "The heavens declare the glory of God; the skies proclaim the work of his hands" (Ps.

19:1). At creation God called the world "good" (Gen. 1). Mankind too was created in a glorious perfection in order to mirror the character of the Creator. Thus the writer of the epistle to the Hebrews, quoting from Psalm 8:4, stated:

> *"You made him a little lower than the angels;*
> *You crowned him with glory and honor*
> *and put everything under his feet."*
> —Heb. 2:7

Genesis tells us that "God created man in his own image, in the image of God he created him; male and female he created them" (Gen. 1:27). So God made man to share his moral perfections and qualities. Man was wonderfully made because he was stamped with the character of his Creator.

God's Glory and the Awfulness of Sin

This brings us to the sad story of the fall of man. The glory of God that was intended to be revealed through the creation has been terribly blighted and marred through sin.

The Bible tells us that the disobedience of Adam brought a curse upon God's creation. God told Adam, "Cursed is the ground because of you" (Gen. 3:17). Now our world is disfigured. Our understanding of the divine purpose—to reveal God's character—is now only a slight glimmer of the glories and beauties grasped by our first parents. Now the creation groans under the weight of divine wrath, awaiting the redemption of the heavens and the earth in the final day (Rom. 8:19-23). What was intended by God to please himself has become a reminder to us that justice demands the punishment of sin, that sin cannot go unpunished.

Adam's rebellion had dire implications for the creation. Driven from God's presence and thrust out into a diabolical world, Adam's very nature was

THE PURPOSE OF CREATION

judged by God. Man was separated from God spiritually, and he suffered an enormous corruption of his character. Instead of the fruit of the Spirit (Gal. 5:22-23), which would mirror the character of God and fulfill man's purpose of glorifying him, man became characterized by the deeds of his newly corrupt nature. His faculties (mind, affections, and will) turned from God's intended purposes to selfish, limited preoccupations. In reality man "exchanged the glory of the immortal God for images made to look like mortal man and birds and animals and reptiles" (Rom. 1:23). He suffered the ruin of his character and with it his freedom, which was his ability to serve God from a pure heart. John Piper has called this "a suicidal exchange of infinite value and beauty for some fleeting, inferior substitute" (*God's Passion for His Glory*, p. 36).

Sin is mankind's willful choice, in spite of the unceasing mercies and kindnesses of God, to refuse to honor him by reflecting his character. God made us for that supreme purpose, but we determined to go the way of our own selfish preoccupations. Any action that does not reflect the character of the Creator in its motive and consequences is sin. It is an assault on God's prerogative to spurn God's glory and act in our own self-interests.

Though sad, this is not the end of the story. The God who desired to see his beauty and excellencies in us will not be defeated in his purposes, though the final restoration of mankind awaits the final re-creation of all things. In Revelation, that final description of the triumph of God over all opposition, God says, "I am making everything new!" (21:5).

FOUR

The Glory of God:
The Chief End of Man

The Chief End of Man Lost

As strange as it may sound initially, to live for
God's glory alone does not denigrate self-worth or
love of self. It only suggests a proper perspective
on the love of self. The Bible presupposes a love of
self, a desire to experience pleasure and avoid
pain, as inherent in the human makeup and as the
ground of ethical imperatives. For example, loving ourselves is often used as a criterion in
Scripture for the love of others. It is an assumed
fact that we do love ourselves, and it is not evil to
do so if it is done rightly. The Bible says, "'Love
your neighbor as yourself'" (Matt. 19:19). Also,
"husbands ought to love their wives as their own
bodies. He who loves his wife loves himself" (Eph.
5:28). Thus Christianity, far from denigrating
human worth, actually presupposes it in some of
its fundamental teachings.

Yet something has tragically blighted and
twisted love of self into a gross perversion of God's
intent for his creatures. The fall of the race into sin
caused love of self to become mere selfishness. What
was lost was a focus outside the self—that is, a love
of God that gave it control and benevolence. Said
Jonathan Edwards, "The ruin which the Fall brought
upon the soul of man consists very much in that he
lost his nobler and more extensive principles, and fell

wholly under the government of self-love. . . . Self-love became absolute master of the soul, the nobler and spiritual principles having taken warning and fled" ("Charity and Its Fruits," *Works*, 8:252-253).

The human desire for happiness is not evil. What is perverse about our quest for happiness is the manner in which we search for it. Natural fallen love errs in thinking the object of loving others to be other than God. The error is that the motive for the expression of love is self-benefit. The Fall caused a restriction of love in the creature; we lost love for God though we retained a love for things and objects. In losing its highest ideal, love became narrow, private, and inward.

As a result, man's love is now the opposite of the true love summarized in 1 Corinthians 13. In turning from God, we lost the only valid definition of true human love and now find ourselves engulfed by a grotesque, distorted vestige of it. Such things as impatience, pride, seeking revenge, envy, and love of evil reveal the awful self-centeredness that has overtaken us. The fruits of the flesh (Gal. 5:19-21) have replaced the fruit of the Spirit (Gal. 5:22-23) that characterized the lives of our first parents.

What Pleasing God Is Not

If it is assumed that God accepts nothing as pleasing to himself except what conforms to the perfections of his absolute righteousness and holiness, can even the highest of noble human endeavors impress God? The psalmist saw the problem when he wrote:

> Who may ascend the hill of the LORD?
>   Who may stand in his holy place?
> He who has clean hands and a pure heart,
>   who does not lift up his soul to an idol
>   or swear by what is false.
>   —Ps. 24:3-4

Jesus echoed the same thought when he said, "Blessed are the pure in heart, for they will see God" (Matt. 5:8). The negative counterpart of our Lord's words would be, "Woe to the impure of heart, for they shall never see God."

Since God is the criteria of his own holiness and I am a sinner, it is impossible for me to please God. The reason is clear: Even the highest of possible human achievements are not devoid of ill motives, whether it be greed, a prideful desire for applause, or something else. There is a shadowed morality in all fallen creatures. Though common morality may be the basis of civil society and the ground for human government, independent of God, it cannot rise to such a level that he could behold his perfections in it.

Common morality, the glue of family and society, is grounded in self-love and the desire to enjoy pleasant circumstances. It is rooted in a desire for one's own happiness, a morality based upon hope of a good return. This is not true virtue because it is self-centered. Both gratitude and anger can be accounted for through self-love alone. The *motive* for an action determines the virtuousness of it, not the action itself. Common morality can be explained without developing an elaborate theory; it is simply part of the structure of our human natures, who we are as God made us. Therefore, an ethic based upon the Golden Rule alone or a God-given moral sense is not truly virtuous in itself. This is so because a moral act done apart from a transcendent object—love for God and his beauty—is a false morality. It is impossible to have a divinely sanctioned morality if God is not the object of and motive for it.

What Pleasing God Means

If one of the central affirmations of true Christianity is that of Romans 11:36 ("For from him and through him and to him are all things. To him be the glory forever! Amen"), it is important that we have a firm understanding of what it means to please God. To state it succinctly, God is only pleased with that which is in perfect agreement with his perfections. God is only glorified in himself either in beholding his innate triune perfections within his own being or observing himself through his creation. Truly pleasing God from the creature's perspective means being like God in moral and spiritual qualities.

The distinction of right from wrong, good from evil, has its ultimate ground in the character of God. Glorifying God, too, is rooted in the being of God. The origin of true virtue must be outside the narrowed, blighted creature; virtue must be given to him from God as a gift. To please God we must be renewed in our characters, which were disoriented by the Fall. This means the vision of God must be restored to us. How could we ever come to reflect a perfection of character that was lost unless such a restoration occurs?

What, then, is true virtue or righteousness? True virtue is rooted in an inward perception of the holiness and beauty of God. It is an outward vision that turns our inward delights and desires away from self for self's advantages to God for God's sake alone. This renewal begins in the human mind as the knowledge of God through the Word of God by the Spirit is revealed to it. It results in the heart's affective perception of the beauty and wonder of God's very being. It emanates from the heart, the seat of man's being, from seeing such a knowledge of God that we desire to be like him. Thus true virtue involves our consent and willingness of heart to love, enjoy, and conform to God's character.

Only a Christian can have true virtue because only a Christian can delight in God for who he is alone. Many say they have a love for God, but their love is only pleasure in God as the giver of good gifts and pleasant circumstances. This type of love is really a love of self because God is not the supreme object of the appreciation. It is merely a love for God as a provider, a Santa Claus; it is not a biblical love.

To place virtue in anything other than a love for God as he is in his holy character and beauty is to have no virtue at all. Moral philosophers and secularists who try to ground moral virtue in the Golden Rule or some corporate ethic will fail even in their most noble endeavors, because the dark side of human nature is not changed by efforts at mere idealism. In fact, the evil of man has a way of resurfacing in the best of circumstances with devastating consequences for humanity. What the philosophers seek is commendable, but the means are inadequate for its accomplishment. Common morality is a narrow preoccupation with self that has no transcendent anchor or defining point.

To glorify God means to have the nature of God restored to us. This can only come through the renewal of the life of God in the soul, and the way to experience this is what the Bible describes as the return of man to God. The core of conversion is the gift from God of a new indwelling principle in the heart of mankind. That principle is the very life of God; it is the love of God. This alone is the ground of true virtue and morality and is the exclusive means for glorifying God. You simply cannot be pleasing to one you are not like!

FIVE

The Glory of God:
The Meaning of Salvation

Some years ago in a little church in a faraway town a little boy sat tormented of soul, unloved (or so he thought), and embittered by the hurts he had already experienced in his few years. Feeling lonely and forsaken, he listened to a message about the utter brokenness of man, which he had no trouble understanding, and the grace of God in sending the Savior, which was wonderful. Suddenly it was as though a light broke forth in his inner being. He understood the gospel story of a dying and redeeming Christ, and he experienced a flood of light into his soul, bringing an unexplainable transformation. Light replaced the darkness, joy the inward fears, love the enshrined heartaches. He had such a new delight in God and Christ that it took years of study to more completely comprehend.

I was that young boy.

In time I learned that what I had experienced was the life-changing experience that the Bible calls "the new birth" or being "born again." And I discovered in the annals of Christian history that I was not alone in this experience. St. Augustine, Martin Luther, Blaise Pascal, Jonathan Edwards, and countless others have described their conversion in similar words—a crucial renewal brought about by the marvelous grace of God through Christ alone. Only through that event, because of the transformation that it brings into our very being, can we glorify God.

An Enrapturing Vision of God

The experience of the grace of God in redemption is a life-changing, infused perception of the beauty and enrapturing excellence of God, caused by the implantation of divine life in the soul. The Bible says that as believers we "participate in the divine nature" (2 Pet. 1:4) and "share in Christ" (Heb. 3:14), and this profoundly transforms the way we think and act.

A glimpse of the magnificence of God in Christ reaches into every facet of our being, touching our minds, hearts, and wills. However, the locus for this transformation is the heart, the deepest inner sphere of the soul. This is why the unsaved are described as "uncircumcised in heart" (Ezek. 44:7) and why God promises to purify his people by writing his law "on their hearts" (Jer. 31:33).

Receiving a new heart means being renewed from the inside out. The divine presence in the inner being gives rise to a subjective sense of the wonder and beauty of God in his mercy and grace, as well as a new disposition or nature. The subjective vision of God is not verifiable. It is a private experience given to us by the Holy Spirit through Scripture, a reality to which we cling in faith. However, the new disposition is discernible because of its effect on our thought life and outward behavior. The first is a personal guide to assurance. The second is available for inspection and is evidence of the inward change for us as well as for others who may observe the effects of the divine life in our souls.

If salvation is the implantation of a new, infinite life in the soul, it must be wholly a work of God. Self-caused effects can never rise above the character or qualities of their cause. "Flesh gives birth to flesh, but the Spirit gives birth to Spirit," Jesus told Nicodemus (John 3:6). Thus, saving grace cannot be caused by the creature. It can only come from God.

Implantation of a New Principle

What precisely is this new principle that is infused into the soul through the miracle of rebirth? This new internal rule is the presence of the Holy Spirit himself in the believer. Ephesians 1:13 tells us that when we were saved, we "were marked in him with a seal, the promised Holy Spirit." The Holy Spirit was given to us as the guarantee of the new life and the evidence of it. Paul stated bluntly in Romans 8:9, "You . . . are controlled not by the sinful nature but by the Spirit, if the Spirit of God lives in you. And if anyone does not have the Spirit of Christ, he does not belong to Christ."

The Holy Spirit is given to believers at the instant of their rebirth. This is why the humblest saint is referred to as "spiritual" or "spiritually-minded." The very life of God is in his soul. The saint's knowledge of redemption is called "spiritual wisdom and understanding" (Col. 1:9); the grace and comforts of God to the saints are referred to as "every spiritual blessing" (Eph. 1:3); a blessing of God to a believer is called a "spiritual gift" (Rom. 1:11). We are not called "saints" because of what we are in ourselves but because of the new life of the Spirit that has been given to us.

What is the manner of the indwelling of the Spirit in the saints of God? Simply put, the Spirit infuses his moral and spiritual character into the innermost recesses of our being. That is, the Holy Spirit manifests himself in the soul by the fruit of the Spirit (Gal. 5:22-23). He himself is the divine principle that produces new desires and affections in believers. He is the character of God infused into our lives.

Evidence of the grace of God in the heart appears in the ninefold fruit of the Spirit. Though believers may have varying degrees of a particular fruit in any set of circumstances, it is not the abundance of the Spirit that is at issue but the mere fact of his presence, which assures us that we have been reborn into a new and remarkably different family. It is interesting that the first fruit of the Spirit in Galatians is "love," a characteristic of God that is also described as the supreme character quality of the saint in 1 Corinthians 13. The Spirit gives us himself, which means that into our being has come "love, joy, peace, patience, kindness, goodness, faithfulness, gentleness, and self-control" (Gal. 5:22-23). It is, therefore, little to be marveled at that God says we have passed out of the kingdom of darkness into the kingdom of his dear Son (Col. 1:13).

The Transformation of Life

The Bible describes salvation as old things passing away and new things replacing them. The former things were the fruits of the flesh, a life-experience described by the apostle Paul as being "separate from Christ, excluded from citizenship in Israel and foreigners to the covenants of the promise, without hope and without God in the world" (Eph. 2:12). Yet the radically transforming grace of God breaks forth in the very next verse where Paul begins a description of the change brought into their lives with the words, "but now in Christ Jesus . . ." The Christian life is a transformed life, because God's character in the person of the Holy Spirit is infused into the believer's soul.

This was illustrated for me in the life of a man I met some time ago. In his days as a marine serving in Vietnam, he was known as a cruel, efficient killer. His lifestyle even before those days made his nickname the epitome of contradiction. He was called "Gentle Ben." However, through the mercies of God he was transformed by grace and was brought into the family of God. As a result of the remarkable changes Christ brought, the thought of his past behavior made him unwilling to keep his old name. So he changed it quite appropriately to "Gently Ben." Redemption changed Ben's character, as it does for all who come to Christ.

It is impossible for unbelievers to glorify God, except in proving his warnings to be just and confessing his Word to be true as they bow to him in the final judgment before being righteously consigned to eternal separation from God and everlasting torment in the lake of fire. However, believers glorify God in the deepest and truest sense, because the character of God has become their possession forever. Since God is only pleased with the perfections that he alone possesses, and since these have been granted to us through the Holy Spirit, the believer can glorify God. God is glorified when he sees himself in the character of the believer.

Three Important Implications

Three implications of this truth call for special notice.

1. *Salvation is the unmerited gift of God.* Since salvation is a divine grace in the soul, cleansing it of the guilt of sin and beginning a process for the removal of sin by the infusion of the Holy Spirit, it cannot be in any sense a work of man. A finite creature simply does not have the power to create an infinite life in the soul. Only God can infuse his life into us. Therefore, all boasting is excluded; salvation is of the Lord alone, and glory and praise belong only to him! While the means of salvation are a mystery, the Bible is clear that we are not redeemed by anything we do. In stressing human responsibility, Arminians have taught that mankind is graciously caused to cooperate with God, that

grace *and* human faith are the components of salvation. However, if human faith is even in the
smallest sense the reason for salvation, there is a
place for boasting.

2. *A Christian will follow Christ.* Because salvation is the transformation of our innermost being,
and because it is out of the desires of the heart that
actions spring, it is forever settled that the believer
is a person who desires to follow the Savior in
moral obedience. It is inconceivable that a person
could fall in love with the Redeemer in the biblical
sense and not long to be conformed to the object of
that affection. When the Holy Spirit comes into the
life of a saint, he infuses his divine character into
that person. Thus, a life devoid of that character,
which is the fruit of the Spirit, is simply not a
Christian life.

3. *Christians will obey God's Law.* In coming to
Christ, the believer is no longer under the Law of
God regarding its function of revealing the righteousness of God and the evil consequences of
moral disobedience, causing him to flee for mercy.
But this does not mean the Christian is free from
the Law of God once he or she comes to Christ.
Because the Law is a revelation of God's holy character, and because his character has been infused in
us by the Holy Spirit, the true believer longs to obey
God's regulations. A Christian is one who has found
that to be truly free is to be enslaved to the dictates
of a Master who is full of love and compassion.

SIX

The Glory of God:
The Making of a Lifestyle

When God redeemed us, he placed his Holy Spirit within us. In that wonderful moment we started upon an unexpected journey that will lead to the day when we are completely conformed to the image of Christ. Paul informed the Philippians that "he who began a good work in you will carry it on to completion until the day of Christ Jesus" (Phil. 1:6).

Using an image from agriculture, the Christian life might be described this way. First, the seed of the new birth is planted in the soil of the believer at regeneration. The Spirit comes to infuse his character in us, and thus the basis is laid whereby God can be glorified in us. Second, with proper nourishment and cultivation the seed sprouts, flowers, and begins to bear fruit. Finally, through constant growth the plant reaches maturity and bears ripe, wholesome fruit. If this stage can be likened to our final maturity that will be brought about in glorification, the second stage can be a metaphor for the believer's growth in Christ or his spiritual progress in greater degrees of conformity to Christ. This is the doctrine of progressive sanctification or the gradual separation of the saint from those things that are out of conformity to the character of God and growth into greater degrees of conformity to him. If the purpose of the believer is the glory of

God alone, and it is, then progressive sanctification should be of paramount importance to us.

Similarly, the Christian's life may be described by the metaphor of a forest. Before God saved us, our lives were dense jungles of trees, wild vines, and weeds. If you were to fly over that forest, you would observe such a perplexity of growth that there would be no clearings. This tangle of vines and trees represents the hold of sin on our lives, and it is universal. However, when God granted us life through Christ and the Spirit came to indwell us, a marvelous change began to take place. Now if you could fly over the jungle of your life, you would observe that there are still vines, trees, and weeds, but there are also clearings, areas in your life where sin no longer dominates. God has begun his reclamation process. The removal of the remaining trees and vines is progressive sanctification. As we struggle against the remnants of the fruits of the flesh, the forest is progressively cleared of tangles. Saints reflect greater and greater degrees of the character of God and thereby glorify him.

The task before every child of God is to root out and destroy the remainders of the sin that once had universal control over him or her. By this means alone can we glorify God.

Personal Godliness

When God regenerates the soul, he causes a radical transformation within it. In short, he reorients the affections and renovates character. Love and joy, as well as the seven other fruits of the Spirit, spring to life. Such things as pride, envy, jealousy, and bitterness receive a mortal, if not yet a final, blow. The wonderful line in the old hymn comes true in experience:

> *Things I loved before have passed away.*
> *Things I love far more have come to stay.*

As a result of our rebirth, we have come to love God for the beauty of his character and not merely as a provider.

This wonderful transformation has many personal features. In essence redemption entails a transformation of the moral nature, and its features are many. These include humility, a tenderness of conscience in regard to offending others and the Lord, an appetite for greater spiritual growth as opposed to personal prominence or personal glory, a longing for the Word of God, and a desire to worship.

Jonathan Edwards wrote a beautiful description of the inner change that comes to the vilest of sinners when God moves in grace to redeem. It is a description of a life that glorifies God alone because it is a life in which God beholds himself.

> The higher the hope is raised, the more there is of this Christian tenderness . . . increase of a reverential fear . . . increase of fear of his displeasure itself . . . the more apt he is to be alarmed with the appearance of moral evil. . . . As he has more holy boldness, so he has less of self-confidence. . . . As he is more sure than others of deliverance from hell, so he has more of a sense of the desert of it. . . . He has the firmest comfort, but the softest heart: richer than others, but poorest of all in spirit: the tallest and strongest saint, but the least and tenderest child among them. ("Treatise on Religious Affections," *Works*, 2:364)

The means for the cultivation of this quality of life have traditionally been divided into two parts. There are things that are vital for positive growth to take place; these are often called works of *vivification*. They include the reading and serious study of the Word of God, the fellowship of the saints, meeting in worship to hear the Word of God, heeding spiritual counsel, and prayer. There is also a negative side to spiritual maturity, the putting to death of the deeds of the flesh (Rom. 8:13), a struggle against sin in our lives so as to root it out or at least minimize its influences over us. This is called *mortification.*

There can be little spiritual growth without a serious endeavor to participate in the means that God has ordained for it.

Public Godliness

Progressive sanctification, a life of mirroring God's character, is far more than personal, private piety, however. If there is not a public dimension of personal growth, there is a serious question whether there is any real growth at all. There simply cannot be a change of moral nature without an accompanying alteration in morals, personal and public.

Genuine redemption in Christ always leads to a life of fruit-bearing for Christ. If the deepest meaning of coming to Christ is a profound, affectionate falling in love with him for his intrinsic excellencies, it is unthinkable that one can truly be in love with him and not want to conform to his desires. How can one lay claim to the presence of the Holy Spirit and not bear the fruit of the Spirit if the presence of the Spirit means the working of his character within the believer?

In a rather classic fashion, Edwards makes the point that as the quality of the tree is determined by its fruit, so is the genuineness of Christian profession:

> Christ nowhere says, ye shall know the tree by its leaves or flowers, or ye shall know men by their talk, or ye shall know them by the manner and air of their speaking, and emphasis and pathos of expression, or by

their speaking feelingly, or by making a very great show by the abundance of talk, or by many tears and affectionate expressions, or by the affections you feel in your heart toward them; by their fruits ye shall know them. ("Treatise on Religious Affections," *Works,* 2:407)

If fruit-bearing is another way of glorifying God, if God beholds himself when he sees himself in both our public and private lives, and if glorifying God is the reason for our creation, then it is vital that our Christianity be as public in nature as it is private in nature. In fact, the two are indistinguishable from God's perspective.

1. *Our Work.* One's perspective on work can be utterly transformed—from the drain of repetitious tasks, whether it be consulting the same people or changing an array of diapers and preparing meals, to the purposeful insight that my work is my gift to God. It is a means whereby I can glorify him. By revealing his character on the road to the office or at a child's athletic or play practices, I can now confidently know that wherever I am and whatever task I am doing, I am doing it for the God who alone I am seeking to honor. Does Christ see himself in my attitudes concerning the work he has given me to do? It is a transforming thought that life is not about money, easy circumstances, or early retirement; it is about God seeing himself in our everyday tasks by how we do them. The apostle Paul wrote, "Whatever you do, work at it with all your heart, as working for the Lord, not for men" (Col. 3:23).

2. *Politics.* A sphere of influence that believers often neglect is that of politics, local and national. Is it bad actively to seek to promote the general good of society through holding public office or seeking to influence its direction? Hardly! True,

there may be inappropriate ways to express concern, as with most activities. Yet, a concern for a greater number of just laws and the promotion of the public good is a wonderful way to glorify God.

This is because God is more vitally interested in the development of godly attitudes and behavior than he is in the particular realm in which it is expressed. The realm is a matter of divine calling, giftedness, training, and opportunity. But it is through our lives and resultant behavior patterns that God beholds himself, not in the tasks that we perform. Therefore, work is not merely about work, and doing good is not merely about doing good. There is a deeper reason for these things that frees us to follow God's direction whatever it may be. One career choice is not inherently superior to another. Rather, each is an opportunity for God to be glorified. Did not Jesus summarize the entire Law by saying that we are to love the Lord and our neighbors as ourselves?

3. *The environment.* Should we be concerned about the polluting of the earth, whether it be the contamination of the soil by factory pollutants or the destruction of the ozone level, increasing the threat of skin cancers? Should we be concerned about the trash that is carelessly tossed along our highways or about public parks being littered with debris from picnics? I think we should. Let me give three reasons related to the glory of God.

First, though God created the world, like us it has suffered the destructive curses of the Fall. As he cares about the restoration of mankind, so he is glorified when his orderliness, beauty, and symmetry are restored to the world. Did not the psalmist say, "The heavens declare the glory of God; the skies proclaim the work of his hands" (Ps. 19:1)? God is glorified when he beholds himself in nature. Should that not motivate us?

Second, God is glorified in seeing his character in our attitudes and actions. Since he is concerned for his creation, he is eminently glorified by our concerns for it also.

Third, we should be concerned for the environment because it is a way to show our care and concern for people. It is important to seek to make this the best of possible worlds so that God's beauty can be seen by unbelievers and believers alike. The beauty of nature points to the beauty of God. The beauty of God, wherever observed, is the means whereby God is glorified.

When I rise in the morning and bow my heart and mind before God, I generally begin to form my thoughts around one question. I ask God, "Will you grant me the privilege of glorifying you today?" I do not begin by discussing the tasks and duties that may fill a particular day because the purpose for living is not duties. Duties, conversations, and deadlines are vehicles by which I am able to display the character of God. However, this is not the end for which God ordains the gift of every new day. God ultimately desires that he would see himself in me each day. Then, at the end of the day when I often in weariness fall into bed, I reserve enough energy to ask another question: "Have you, O God, seen yourself in what I said, thought, and did today? Did I care for others the way you would have?" Through these questions I find the answers to the greatest of all life's questions: Did I fulfill my destiny today? Did I glorify God? Did God see his character in my attitudes and actions?

SEVEN

A Call to a God-Centered Vision

A way to discover the ultimate meaning of temporal things is to determine what they will look like in their final state of existence. For example, what will creation be like when time turns into eternity? In eternity, the creation, so horribly disfigured by the Adamic rebellion and in spite of our serious attempts to bring it once again into subjection to God, will only then be what God originally purposed for it. The Bible says that now the creation is "groaning" as it awaits its redemption (Rom. 8:22). The description of the new heavens and the new earth in Revelation and certain other prophetic passages is one of perfect beauty and harmony. The heavens will perfectly proclaim the excellencies and beauties of God, and the earth will flower forth in praise and adoration of him alone. In the end creation will praise him. This in itself is sufficient to tell us that the original purpose of creation was the same. God does not purpose something that does not eventuate.

To God be the glory alone!

According to the Bible, the destiny of the human race is the same as that of the creation. Redeemed men and women throughout eternity will praise and worship God in the perfections of their glorified natures. In Revelation John wrote:

Then I heard every creature in heaven and on earth and under the earth and on the sea, and all that is in them, singing:

"To him who sits on the throne and to the Lamb be praise and honor and glory and power, for ever and ever!"

The four living creatures said, "Amen," and the elders fell down and worshiped.
—Rev. 5:13-14

When time shall be no more, when temporal things fold into eternity and the cares and concerns that now consume us end, God alone will continue to be glorified. The reason for our lives is just this: God desires to behold himself in us. He is glorified not by the creature himself but by himself shining forth through the creature. This is the essence of our call to a radical vision of the glory of God alone.

In his commentary on Romans, John Calvin had some perceptive insights on Romans 11:36, the passage that has formed the central thought of this booklet. He wrote of God:

> He is the source of all things in that they have proceeded from him; he is the Creator. He is the agent through whom all things subsist and are directed to their proper end. And he is the last end to whose glory all things redound. The apostle is thinking of all that comes within the created and providential order. God is the Alpha and Omega, the beginning and the end, the first and the last. . . . And to him must not only glory be ascribed; to him all glory will redound.

So it will be. And so we say, To God alone be *all* the glory.

FOR FURTHER
READING

Boston, Thomas. *Human Nature in Its Four-Fold State,* 1743. Carlisle, Pa: Banner of Truth Trust, 1989.

Bridges, Jerry. *Trusting God: Even When It Hurts.* Colorado Springs, Colo: NavPress, 1989.

Charnock, Stephen. *The Existence and Attributes of God,* 1797. Reprint Minneapolis: Klock & Klock, 1977.

Edwards, Jonathan. *Treatise on Religious Affections,* 1746. Carlisle, Pa: Banner of Truth Trust, 1997.

——. *The Works of Jonathan Edwards.* 17 volumes. New Haven, Conn.: Yale University Press, 1959-present.

Owen, John. "On Communion with God," in *The Collected Works of John Owen,* vol. 3, 1850-1853. London: Banner of Truth Trust, 1966.

Pink, Arthur W. *The Sovereignty of God,* 1928. Carlisle, Pa: Banner of Truth Trust, 1972.

Piper, John. *God's Passion for His Glory.* Wheaton, Ill.: Crossway Books, 1998.

Ryle, John Charles. *Holiness: Its Nature, Hindrances, Difficulties and Roots.* Westwood, N.J.: Fleming H. Revell, n.d.

Sproul, R. C. *Grace Unknown: The Heart of Reformed Theology.* Grand Rapids, Mich.: Baker, 1997.

Whitney, Donald S. *Spiritual Disciplines for the Christian Life.* Colorado Springs, Colo: NavPress, 1992.